playmobil®

JOURNEY AROUND THE
WORLD

Richard Unglik

Dear readers,

I was inspired to make an old dream come true — to go on a tour of the world and share it with you in a travelogue and map.

Unfortunately, I wasn't able to visit every country, region, and city on this planet — there are way too many, and a whole lifetime would never be enough! So I selected the places that stood out, the ones I found the most beautiful and the most picturesque.

During my journey, I was extremely fortunate to meet another globe-trotter, Bruno Peeters, better known as Brubil.

We met at various stages along the trip and even had the joy of visiting a few countries together.

I can't wait to share my voyage with you... May your journey be just as beautiful and fun!

I am dedicating this book to all the doctors who took care of me during this tour of the world: Dr. Colin Charpy, Dr. Gibault Genty, Dr. Barthélemy, Dr. Vaillant, Aude, and Julie.

Richard Unglik

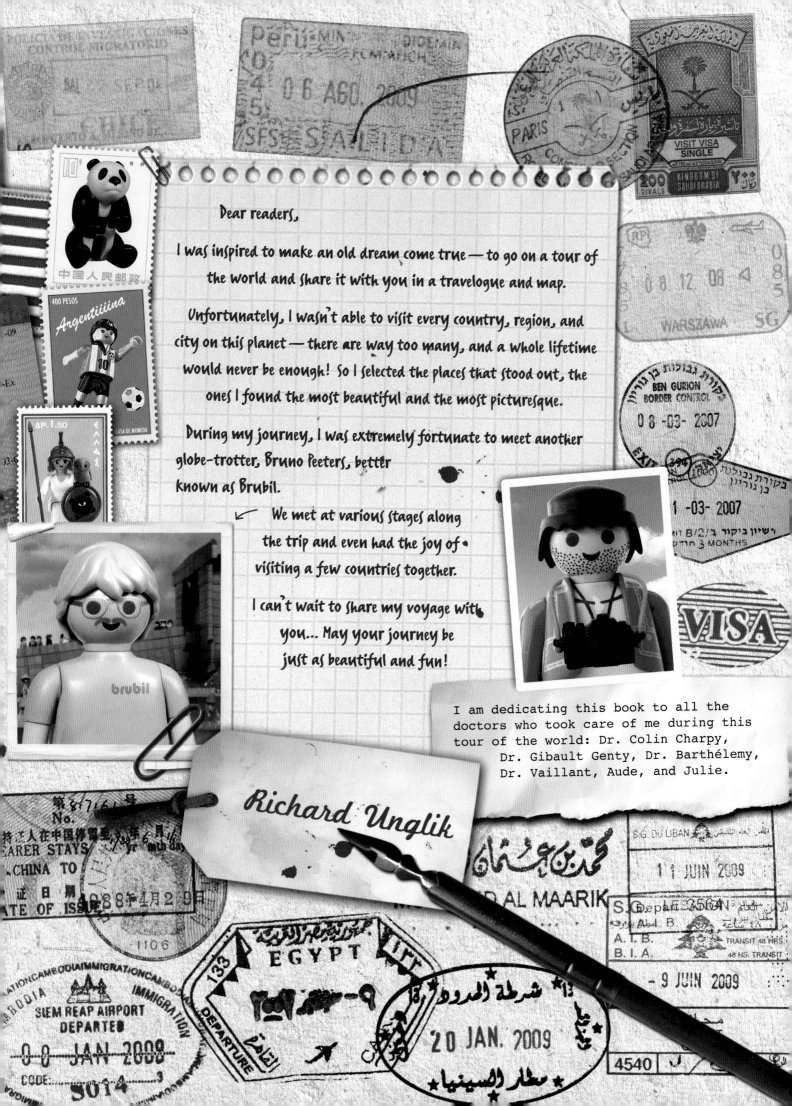

DEUTSCHLAND

I will start in Germany since it is Playmobil's native country! The Fun Park in Nuremberg is a must-see. Playmobil was created in 1974, thanks to the imagination of Hans Beck (1929-2009). They have been spreading across the world ever since, with growing success.

Throughout the 20th century, Germany's history was stained with tragedies and unrest: two world wars and the most violent dictatorship in mankind's history. With the fall of the infamous Berlin Wall in November 1989, the curse seemed to come to an end at last, and Germany could finally — and peacefully — reunite.

Today, Germany shines in sports. Michael Schumacher is one of the greatest Formula 1 champions, and the national German soccer team ranks among the most talented worldwide.

Michael Schumacher: A German race car driver, born in 1969. With 7 world champion titles in Formula 1 and 91 Grand Prix victories, he is considered one of the best race car drivers of all time, and he has the most impressive track record in the sport.

Richard Wagner
Bayreuther Festspiele

Marlene Dietrich: An actress and singer (1901-1992). In 1930, the movie *The Blue Angel* gave her instant worldwide fame. She fled from Nazi Germany in 1937 and became an American citizen.

Richard Wagner: A German composer (1813-1883). A genius with an unusually universal appeal, Wagner is famous in Western music history for his operas, *The Flying Dutchman, Tristan and Isolde*, and others. He challenged the musical criteria of his time in order to reach "total work of art."

Der fliegende Holländer

8. 9. und 10. September
Festspielhaus

As music lovers know, Germany is a great destination for those who are fans of classical music. Once a year, the Bayreuth Festival draws Wagner opera enthusiasts. As for Bach, Beethoven, or Brahms, music recitals can be found pretty much everywhere in Germany.

But Germany is also a great place for beer enthusiasts: they gather once a year in Munich at "Oktoberfest," the famous beer festival. Prosit (cheers)!

Ludwig van Beethoven

Deutsche Bundespost 150
Richard Wagner

MÜNCHEN

Paris is my city. I was born here, I grew up here, and I know its most secret corners. So my world tour is the perfect occasion to discover a facet of the French capital I'm not used to: Paris for "tourists." Quite an adventure!

10 a.m.: Visit The Louvre museum with its famous Mona Lisa and graceful Venus de Milo. But Paris is also the capital of upscale fashion design.

I couldn't possibly miss the shops of Avenue Montaigne. Exhausted, my legs feeling like jelly, it's time for dinner in one of the many restaurants dedicated to the French culinary arts.

Nightfall is the most magical time. The Eiffel Tower sparkles with thousands of lights; no wonder Paris is called "The City of Lights!"

I end the day with a celebratory dinner at Moulin Rouge, where I have champagne and watch French cancan dancers.

PARIS

VENDREDI
9

8 — 8
9 — 9
10 10 a.m.
Visit The Louvre
11 — 11
12 — 12
13 — 13
14 Shopping
Avenue
15 Montaigne 15
16 — 16
17 — 17
18 Eiffel Tower
19 — 19
20 10 p.m.
21 Dinner at
Moulin Rouge!!!

Mona Lisa: A famous portrait painted by Leonardo da Vinci between 1503 and 1506. It is the most famous painting in the world because it represents a defining point in the art of the Renaissance portrait. It is also the most widely seen work of art at The Louvre, drawing millions of admirers who are intrigued by Mona Lisa's mysterious smile.

The *Venus de Milo*

RESTAURANT
chez Marcel

30, avenue des Champs-Elysées -78008 Paris

Eiffel Tower: A metal tower built by Gustave Eiffel for the 1889 World Fair. Originally 984 feet (310 meters) high, and later extended thanks to a handful of antennas, it stands today at 1,063 feet (324 meters). Located near the banks of the river Seine, this monument has come to symbolize Paris. With nearly 7 million visitors a year, it is one of the most visited sites in the world.

ELLE
MAGAZINE

SPÉCIAL HAUTE COUTURE

PARIS, VILLE DE LA MODE

KARL L.
INTERVIEW EXCLUSIVE

The capital of high-end fashion, Paris welcomes the most acclaimed designers in the world.

In Montmartre, the quarter is filled with cabarets where people dance the French cancan, giving Paris its slightly racy reputation.

Cabinet extra dry 1992

Belgium consists of two types of people: the Flemish, who live in the north and speak Dutch, and the Walloons who live in the south and speak French. This bilingualism can sometimes pose problems.

In the plat pays (flat country), humor and self-deprecation are an art form; no wonder Belgium is the "mecca" of bande dessinée — a type of comic book found in Belgium and France — and surrealism.

Countless comic book heroes were born in Belgium, and the most famous publishing houses are headquartered there.

As for surrealism, who could represent it better than painter René Magritte?

René Magritte: A Belgian painter (1898–1967) who was a leading figure of the surrealist artistic movement.

Take a good look at this Magritte painting: Is the horse-back rider in front of the tree or behind it? She is both in front AND behind! This is what surrealism is — a twist on reality.

161635
1 TOEGANG
VAN GOGH MUSEUM

.32 231 023
Rijksmuseum

Vermeer (1632-1675) and Van Gogh (1853-1890) are major Dutch artists: I couldn't possibly visit Amsterdam without admiring their artwork in the city's museums!

The Netherlands is often inaccurately called Holland, even by the Dutch themselves. As a matter of fact, Holland is just one of the Netherlands' regions. Holland is actually home to Netherlands' main cities: The Hague, Amsterdam, and Rotterdam.

The Netherlands has one of the lowest altitudes of all the countries in the world. One-quarter of the country is below sea level. This is why the Dutch have built an impressive network of dikes and polders. A polder is an artificial area of land that is lower than sea level.

The queen of the Netherlands is named Beatrix. But the Dutch have two other little "queens" they are extremely proud of—bicycles and tulips.

Because of the strong winds that blow across its land, ancient windmills break up the Netherlands' landscape, which gives it a unique pastoral charm.

United Kingdom

Changing of the guards in front of Buckingham Palace

Union Jack: The United Kingdom's flag since 1801. It is composed of the English St. George's cross (red on a white background), the Scottish St. Andrew's cross (white on a blue background), and the Irish St. Patrick's cross (red).

THE BEATLES

The Beatles: A British music band from Liverpool, made up of John Lennon, Paul McCartney, George Harrison, and Ringo Starr. With the highest record sales in history, the Beatles remain one of the most popular pop bands in the world, in spite of their separation in 1970.

With its world-famous queen, Buckingham Palace, rock 'n' roll bands, businessmen in bowler hats, and men in kilts playing bagpipes — not to mention Shakespearean actors waving skulls, lakes swarming with monsters next to haunted castles, its fearless secret agents, and its famous detective for whom everything is just so "elementary" (Sherlock Holmes) — the United Kingdom is probably the most exciting of all!

The United Kingdom includes a number of countries that are unique from one another: England, Ireland, Scotland, and Wales. The most fun way to appreciate the identity of each of these countries is to spend an evening at the "pub," a typical bar where Brits love to gather after a hard day of work.

Hamlet: One of the most famous tragedies written by William Shakespeare (1564–1616). The play, which takes place in Denmark, relates how Prince Hamlet avenges his father, who was assassinated and robbed of his throne by a usurper. In this play, Hamlet utters the famous question: "To be or not to be?"

When the world is in danger, England sends its best secret agent to the rescue: Bond, James Bond. Code name: 007

English Pub
The London City
9 Regent St.
London

the **Patrick's Irish Pub**
71, Bishop Street, Dublin

the **MacLeod's Scottish Pub**
Glasgow   Scotland

↑
Aileen,
an Irish
friend

...day
forever

My friend McIntosh, playing bagpipes in front of Nessie, the Loch Ness Monster.

The Adventures of Sherlock Holmes

CONAN DOYLE

For more than a thousand years, a road in Spain has led pilgrims to Santiago de Compostela.

I am here for a different kind of pilgrimage, however. With an equally strong excitement, I came to see two painters I greatly admire: Picasso (1881-1973) and Dalí (1904-1989).

ESPAÑA

Salvador Dalí admiring his wife, Gala.

Don Quixote: He is the hero of *El Ingenioso Hidalgo Don Quijote de la Mancha* (The Ingenious Gentleman Don Quixote of La Mancha), a novel written by Miguel de Cervantes in 1605. Wearing makeshift armor, riding an old mare named Rossinante, and helped by Sancho Panza—a stupid servant whose only motivation is to eat—Don Quixote is an impractical and silly character determined to be a vigilant knight. The most well-known chapter in the novel describes Don Quixote's battle against windmills, which he believes are giants!

Picasso painting *Guernica* (1937).

In the south of Spain, Andalucia is home to cities rich with history: Seville, Cordoba, Granada.

It is also the land of flamenco and bullfighting.

Final pass (the third act of a bullfight) in the splendid arenas of Seville. Facing the *toro* (bull), the matador shakes his red cape, or *muleta*.

Painted by Michelangelo between 1508 and 1512, the ceiling of the Sistine Chapel, at the Vatican, depicts God creating Adam.

Vatican: The residence of the popes in Rome. Measuring 44 "hectares" (0.17 square miles or 0.44 square kilometers), and with only 824 inhabitants, it is the smallest independent state in the world.

ITALIA

la casa dei gela
Italian gelato at Gustimo di R

Piazza del Colosseo

Where does Italy's eternal charm come from? Is it the majesty of the Roman ruins? The beauty of its Renaissance paintings? How about the elegance of its people? Or the pasta and pizzas, which are the best in the world? And did I mention its colorful ice cream? Or could it simply be the Italians' happy and charming dispositions?

In the streets of Rome, pedestrians, scooters, tiny cars, and fancy sports cars share the road.

BC·909XM

Via de Palazzo o de Canonica
Venezia

Venice is an ancient, fanciful city that captivates visitors and brings up powerful emotions. It is mesmerizing, a true architectural jewel. Built on a laguna—a narrow, shallow body of water—along the coastline of the Adriatic Sea, Venice is a puzzle of 118 islands connected by 409 bridges and 160 canals. You won't find any cars here. People walk everywhere through a maze of incredibly charming streets, or they take a romantic gondola ride.

Of course, when in Venice, the carnival is an absolute must. During the month of February, all the Venetians wear their most beautiful masks and costumes. For a whole week, you may run into popular Italian characters, such as Columbine, Harlequin, Pulcinella, and Casanova in the narrow streets of this city.

In front of the Grand Canal in Venice

The lovely Torgon ski resort, where I used to go on school field trips as a child.

Alphorn: A long horn used by shepherds to communicate with each other. Some ca[n] reach up to 16 feet (5 meters) long.

I've always loved going to Switzerland on vacation. It's such a beautiful, mountainous country. In the winter, people ski down the snow-covered slopes, and at night they enjoy fondue or raclette, a yummy dish of melted cheese, with dried meat called viande des Grisons. If you wander in the lovely pastures during the summer, you will hear the sound of horns and bells and find yourself surrounded by cows and marmots.

And all year long, people sip delicious chocolate milk. It is a slow-paced life, punctuated by the cuckoos of very precise clocks!

William Tell is the great legendary figure of Switzerland. He is said to have lived in the Canton of Uri at the beginning of the 14th century, when Switzerland was under Austrian rule. He challenged the local governor, who dared him to shoot a crossbow arrow, aiming at an apple placed on his son's head. Without skipping a beat, William Tell shot his arrow right on the mark. He became the hero of Swiss independence, and later on, of the principle of federalism, so dear to the Swiss.

In fact, aside from maintaining a neutral stance toward the affairs of the world (since 1850), Switzerland is known for being a direct democracy (votes by a show of hand are common), and the 26 cantons (or states) are each independent within their own confederation.

Another unique trait of Switzerland is its banking confidentiality, which is almost impenetrable and has turned this tiny country into the greatest bank in the world.

CHOCOLAT AU LAIT

TRADITION SUISSE

POIDS NET 115g

Edelweiss: A white flower that grows in the Alps above 4,200 feet (1300 meters).

Scandinavia

This land, at the far north of Europe, is composed of four countries: Denmark, Sweden, Norway, and Finland.

In Denmark, the lovely statue of The Little Mermaid watches over Copenhagen, its capital city. It reminds bystanders that the author of the famous tale (written in 1835), Hans Christian Andersen, was Danish.

Sweden, a vast expanse of pine forests, specializes in wood products and furniture manufacturing.

Norway, with its long, jagged coastline and numerous cliffs, has deep ties with the sea, owing to its Viking roots. Its merchant fleet ranks fourth in the world, and it is one of the leading nations in fishing for herring, cod, mackerel, and salmon.

And here I am now in Finland. This country has thousands of lakes and ice deserts. Led by our Sami guide in a sleigh pulled by six reindeer, we discover the magnificent aurora borealis, or Northern Lights. I would love to meet Santa Claus: I heard he lives in Finland, right next to the Arctic Circle!

The Little Mermaid in the port of Copenhagen.

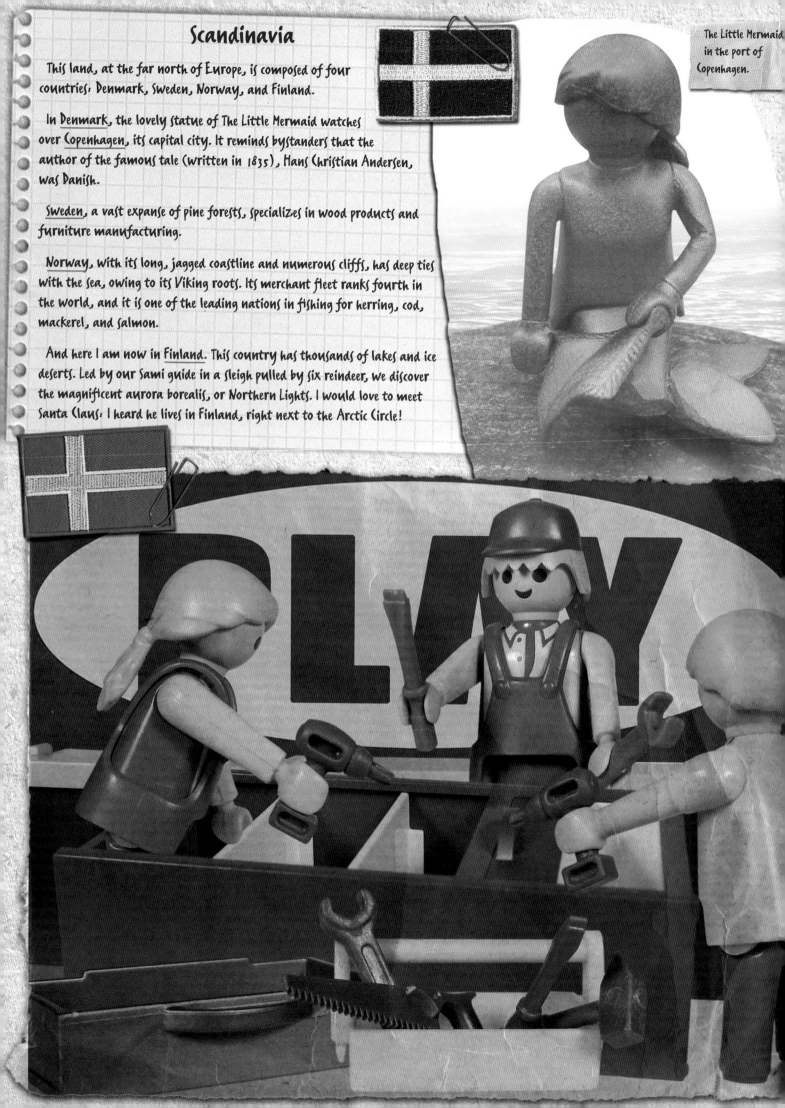

An aurora borealis is a nocturnal light phenomenon that sometimes takes place beyond the Arctic Circle. When it happens, the sky takes on beautiful, otherworldly hues.

Russia is the largest country in the world. More than 5,590 miles (9,000 km) long, it extends across two continents, from the European border to the far eastern side of Asia.

Россия

It's amazing to see how the Slavic soul is still very much alive in Russia. The Slavic soul can be described as a subtle blend of joy, melancholy, and pessimism tinged with fatalism, which is so well conveyed by Russian music.

CIRCUS MOSCOU

Created in 1702 by order of the Czar, the Circus of Moscow is considered the best and most spectacular in the world.

Caviar: Salted sturgeon eggs produced on the shores of the Caspian Sea.

Matriochka: A series of dolls decreasing in size, placed into one another. The word "matriochka" derives from Matriona, a Russian first name that typically evokes a big, strong countrywoman.

The Russian Orthodox Church dates back to the baptism of Prince Vladimir the 1st of Kiev in 988.

Prince Vladimir, who wanted to choose a new religion, sent ambassadors to several different nations in order to learn how they worshiped God.

He chose Byzantine Christianity because of the beauty of the ceremonies. This is why liturgy and art in the Russian Orthodox Church (especially the icons) have so much in common with Byzantine art.

Today, Kiev is the capital of Ukraine, but for the Orthodox Church, it is the equivalent of Rome to Catholicism.

I spend a few days in Romania, in the region called Transylvania. A gypsy camp warmly welcomes me. Gypsies (another name for "Roma") originally came from India. They settled in Eastern Europe about a thousand years ago. What sets them apart is that they are not settled; they are a nomadic people who move frequently with their caravans. In the Middle Ages, they were famous throughout Europe for fearlessly handling and showing tamed bears during street performances.

Transylvania is home to the legendary Count Dracula. Rumor has it that his ancestor was Prince Vlad Tepes Dracul, a bloodthirsty aristocrat who lived in the 15th century.

I am very excited as I stand at the gates of Athens, the capital of Greece — this is the cradle of European civilization!

On my way to the Acropolis, I remember the great thinkers of the 5th century BC, Socrates and Plato, the founders of philosophy; Pythagoras, the creator of geometry; Sophocles, who invented theater; Anaximander, the first to think that the earth may be round and revolve around the sun; Homer, whose Iliad and Odyssey enchanted my childhood...

Not to mention all the gods and the titans who still live in my imagination: Zeus, god of gods; Athena, goddess of wisdom; Poseidon, ruler of the seas; Atlas, who carries the earth above his shoulders; Chronos, the terrible master of time; Hermes and Apollo...and last but not least, the Muses.

Ulysses: One of the most famous heroes of Greek mythology. A particularly cunning warrior, it was he who schemed to build the Trojan horse that allowed the Greeks to defeat the Trojans. A thousand dangers still awaited him on his way home, including the infamous sirens.

Athena: The Greek goddess of wisdom. She is represented armed and accompanied by an owl. She was the protector of Athens, the city that bears her name in her honor.

The ancient Greeks created the Olympic games. Every four years, they gathered in Olympia to enter athletic competitions in honor of Zeus. The competitions included running, long jump, spear throwing, disc throwing, and wrestling.

Athens

The Acropolis
Built in the center of Athens, the Acropolis (or "High City") was the religious center of Greek antiquity—it was a vast sanctuary dedicated to the worship of the goddess Athena and many other gods. Several temples were erected here, including the Parthenon, the Erechtheion, and the temple of Athena Nike.

MINOTAURE
NIGHT CLUB

Ελευθερίου Βενιζέλου 10,
Αθήνα 10671 - 210-3642160

The Greeks gave up polytheism in the 4th century, when the Roman Emperor Constantine converted to Christianity. Today, they are mostly Orthodox, and the priests, who dress in black, are called popes.

ירושלים

"Next year in Jerusalem." For twenty centuries, Jews all over the world have repeated this mantra, ever since the Romans chased them from Jerusalem in the year 70 and their temple was destroyed. Today, all that is left of the destroyed temple is the wall where Jews come to pray. It is called the Wailing Wall.

Jerusalem is considered a holy city by the three monotheistic religions: for Jews, it is where Abraham's sacrifice took place; for Christians, it is the place of the passion and resurrection of Christ; for Muslims, it is the town where Muhammad went to heaven. As you can imagine, these various claims cause rivalry issues in the neighborhood!

ISRAEL

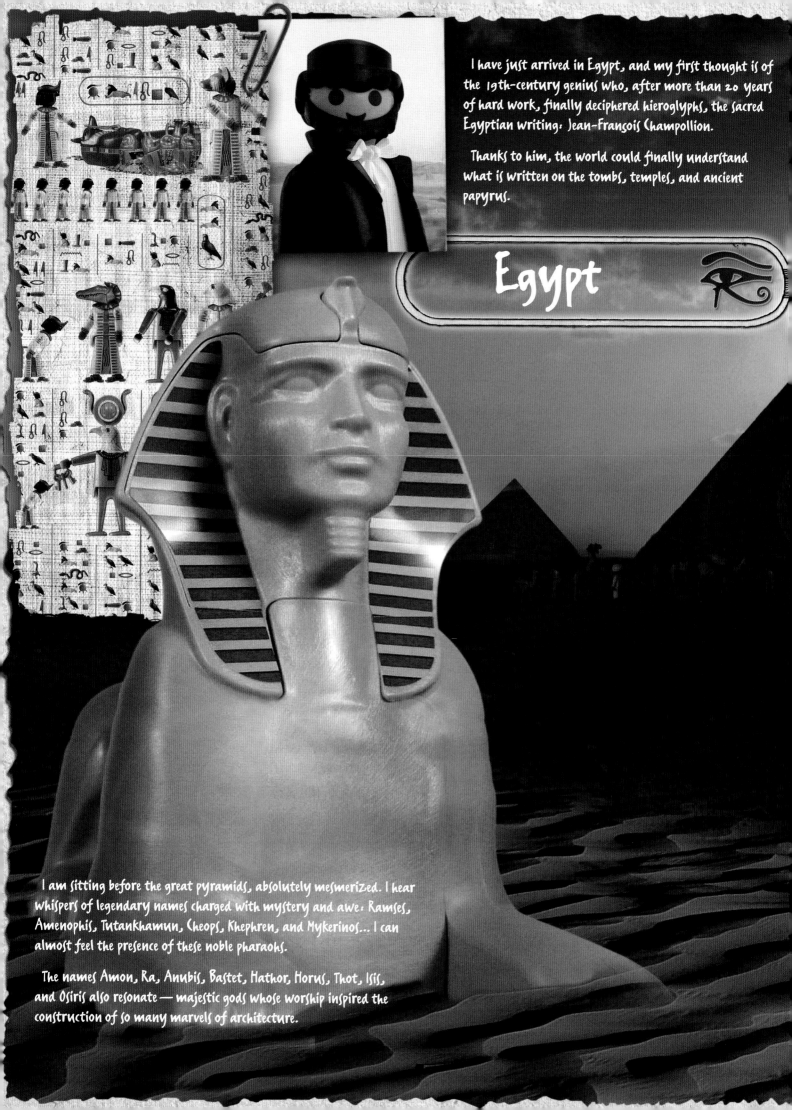

I have just arrived in Egypt, and my first thought is of the 19th-century genius who, after more than 20 years of hard work, finally deciphered hieroglyphs, the sacred Egyptian writing: Jean-François Champollion.

Thanks to him, the world could finally understand what is written on the tombs, temples, and ancient papyrus.

Egypt

I am sitting before the great pyramids, absolutely mesmerized. I hear whispers of legendary names charged with mystery and awe: Ramses, Amenophis, Tutankhamun, Cheops, Khephren, and Mykerinos... I can almost feel the presence of these noble pharaohs.

The names Amon, Ra, Anubis, Bastet, Hathor, Horus, Thot, Isis, and Osiris also resonate — majestic gods whose worship inspired the construction of so many marvels of architecture.

Ever since it arose at the dawn of human history five thousand years ago, Egypt, the land of pharaohs, has fascinated all who travel along its great river: the Nile.

Travelers have always marveled at this majestic civilization, with its temples, colossal sculptures, hieroglyphs, and mysterious mummies locked inside their tombs.

Pharaohs believed another life awaited them after death. So they made sure to pile up their tombs with everything they might need in the afterlife, including their precious belongings!

Alas, grave robbers did not hesitate to violate the burial sites, eager to commit crimes for the gold they were sure to find.

Mali

I am spending a few days in a little village in Mali. Its inhabitants, the Bambara, are particularly welcoming and warm. While Fatoumata and Bintou prepare a delicious "mafé" dish, chatting in front of their hut, their husbands Amadou and Adama are cutting wood they will use to make furniture for a beautiful European-style house.

Mamoutou and Seyba, two cousins from the Kouyaté family, are just returning from hunting wild boar.

Hamidou, the richest man in the village, thanks to his little herd of goats, is watching a soccer game on TV — with his satellite antenna, he can watch channels from all over the world!

The children are playing: Ismael, Samba, and Sotigui like soccer. Their dream is to join the national team, The Eagles of Mali, and to have careers as glorious as Mahamadou Diarra, their idol. Meanwhile, Moussa practices stilt-walking.

Many Mali people are poor, but it doesn't stop them from living happily.

Sub-Saharan Africa

The Sub-Saharan part of this continent is the half that is located below the Sahara.

Composed of 48 countries, Sub-Saharan Africa is rich in natural resources, such as gold, precious gemstones, and wood. Despite this, it is a very poor land. Hunger, drought, and disease affect the daily life of many of its people.

This continent also has highly unstable political regimes and is plagued by numerous civil wars.

Despite its many hardships, however, it thrives on a rich array of traditions and colorful, cultural features. An incredible number of languages and dialects are spoken here: Bambara, Soninke, Dioula, Maasai, Swahili, Bemba, Zulu, Peul, Wolof, Bantu, etc. Something else that makes Sub-Saharan Africa unique is that it is the cradle of humanity. It is the birthplace of a tiny Australopithecus woman, some six million years ago—our very distant ancestor, whom we call Lucy…

VOTE FOR GÉRARD TOUMORÉ

A CANDIDATE WITH COMPETENCE, EXPERIENCE, CREDIBILITY, AND INTEGRITY FOR THE PRESIDENCY OF THE REPUBLIC

REPUBLIEK VAN SUID-AFRIKA
5c
REPUBLIC OF SOUTH AFRICA

KENYA
ORIGINS OF MANKIND
3C

Traditional Musical Instruments
15c
Zimbabwe
1991

African Mask: Mask-making is one of the most well-known expressions of African art. Masks are present at every step of religious life. They are carved in many different materials, although wood is the most preferred.

Diane Fossey: An American ethologist (1932-1985) who specialized in the study of mountain gorillas. Her commitment to the preservation of this species cost her her life—she was murdered by poachers in Rwanda.

Diane Fossey filming a female gorilla (1983).

The African Fauna

I first discovered African animals through Tarzan movies and Diane Fossey's book, Gorillas in the Mist.

So imagine my emotion when I finally saw these formidable creatures up close!

It is unfortunate that such a rich fauna (animal group) must be contained in natural reserves. Throughout the 19th century and a good part of the 20th, the disastrous fashion of safaris and poaching extinguished most of the wild species. In response to the state of emergency, huge wildlife sanctuaries were created where animals could be protected and safely live and reproduce.

Kenya's natural reserves are the most beautiful, and they are home to an impressive population of wild animals: lions, rhinos, elephants, zebras, giraffes, gnus, hyenas, hippopotamus, gazelles, ostriches, and delightful pink flamingos...

Arabia is a vast desert peninsula bordered by the Red Sea and the Gulf of Aqaba on the western side, the Gulf of Aden on the southwestern side, the Indian Ocean on the southern side, the Arabian Sea on the southeastern side, and the Gulf of Oman and the Persian Gulf on the eastern side.

It is made up of seven states. Saudi Arabia, Yemen, Oman, Qatar, the United Arab Emirates, Kuwait, and Bahrain. Arabia owes its impressive wealth to its huge oil deposits, the "black oil," without which the modern world would not be the same. Oil provides the vast majority of liquid fuels and is widely used in the plastics industry.

Mosque: A place of worship where Muslims gather for group prayer. It is adorned with several towers, or minarets. From the top of the minarets, the muezzin calls the people to prayer. The worshipers pray barefoot, their foreheads on the ground, kneeling toward Mecca, the town where Muhammad was born, and the holiest sanctuary of Islam.

Arabia is the cradle of Islam. It is the birthplace of the prophet Muhammad in the year 570. In 610, he received his divine revelation through the voice of Archangel Gabriel in the Hira Cave, after which he created the last monotheistic religion. The Quran, the sacred book of Islam, recalls the stages of this epic saga.

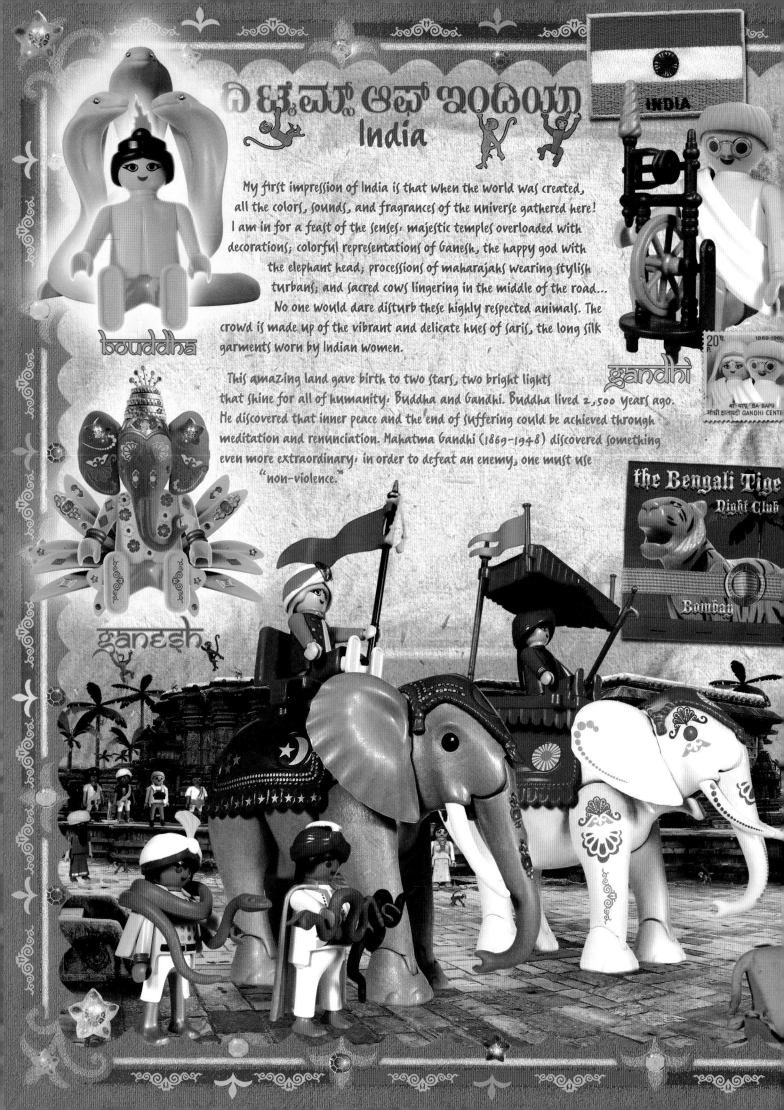

ಎಟ್ಮ್ ಆಫ್ ಇಂಡಿಯ
India

bouddha

My first impression of India is that when the world was created, all the colors, sounds, and fragrances of the universe gathered here! I am in for a feast of the senses: majestic temples overloaded with decorations; colorful representations of Ganesh, the happy god with the elephant head; processions of maharajahs wearing stylish turbans; and sacred cows lingering in the middle of the road... No one would dare disturb these highly respected animals. The crowd is made up of the vibrant and delicate hues of saris, the long silk garments worn by Indian women.

This amazing land gave birth to two stars, two bright lights that shine for all of humanity: Buddha and Gandhi. Buddha lived 2,500 years ago. He discovered that inner peace and the end of suffering could be achieved through meditation and renunciation. Mahatma Gandhi (1869-1948) discovered something even more extraordinary: in order to defeat an enemy, one must use "non-violence."

INDIA

gandhi

ganesh

the Bengali Tiger
Night Club

Bombay

Funerary Pyre in the Ganges

The Ganges is the sacred river of the Hindus. It is a source of regeneration for those who bathe in its waters. When death occurs, great funerary pyres are set up on the river, because dispersing the ashes in the Ganges may bring a better future life. It is said that the river's source is in the hair of Shiva, the god of death and rebirth.

Several sacred Hindu sites are located alongside the Ganges' riverbanks, such as Benares. On its docks, Ghats, who are wise Sadhus with long beards, are in such a state of renunciation that they forget their bodies and are able to walk on burning embers or lie down on a plank lined with nails for days without moving or eating!

Shiva

Om: A Sanskrit syllable found in Hinduism Buddhism. This syllable is considered to be original, primordial sound, around which the universe itself is structured.

Symbol representing the Om syllable.

Lama: A priest or religious figure in Tibet. The Dalai Lama (literally, the Great Lama) is the supreme leader of Tibetan Buddhism.

Lamasery: A Buddhist temple where lamas live.

Before climbing the Himalayas, a peaceful retreat for a few days in a lamasery in Lhasa is a great idea.

A strange chant envelops the monastery:

"Ommmmmmmmmmmm."

The Himalayas are home to more than 60 ethnic groups and casts: the Shetris, the Bahun, the Newars, the Sherpas, and others.

But it is in Kathmandu, the political and religious capital of Nepal, that I meet the strangest of all ethnic groups: the hippies.

In search of serenity, they fled from the United States and Europe in the 70s and settled here. Some of them never returned to their countries of origin!

Kathmandu

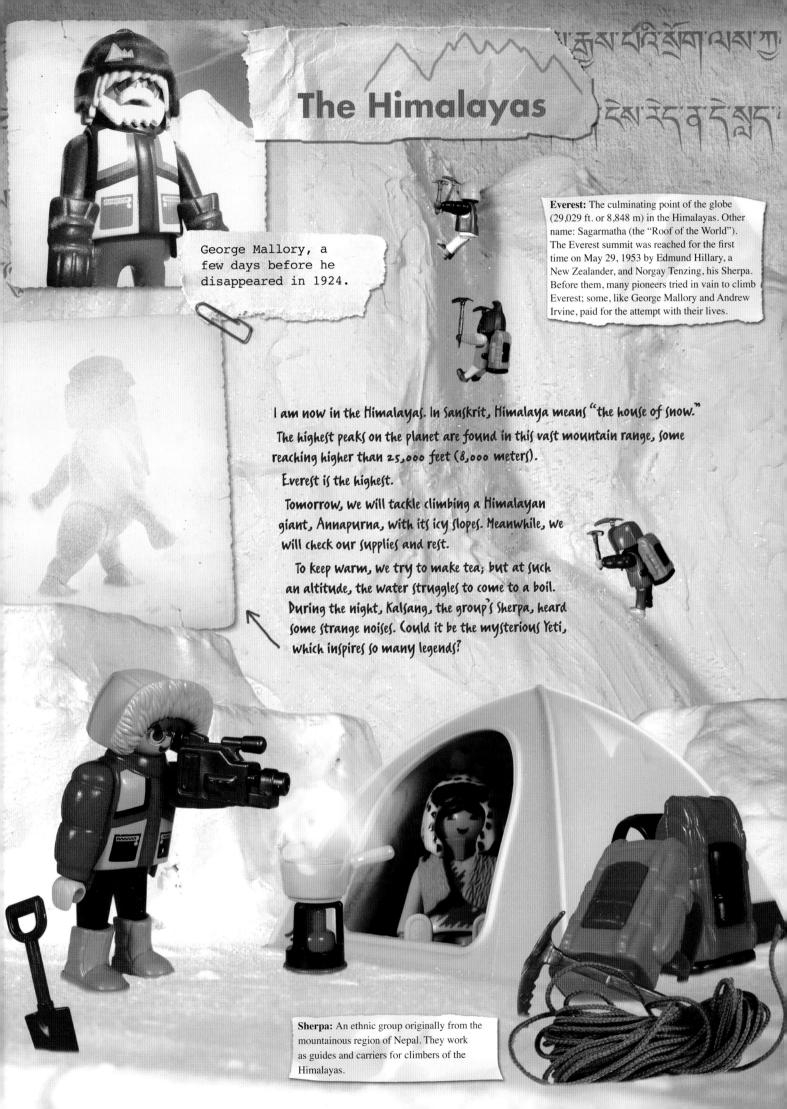

The Himalayas

George Mallory, a few days before he disappeared in 1924.

Everest: The culminating point of the globe (29,029 ft. or 8,848 m) in the Himalayas. Other name: Sagarmatha (the "Roof of the World"). The Everest summit was reached for the first time on May 29, 1953 by Edmund Hillary, a New Zealander, and Norgay Tenzing, his Sherpa. Before them, many pioneers tried in vain to climb Everest; some, like George Mallory and Andrew Irvine, paid for the attempt with their lives.

I am now in the Himalayas. In Sanskrit, Himalaya means "the house of snow."

The highest peaks on the planet are found in this vast mountain range, some reaching higher than 25,000 feet (8,000 meters).

Everest is the highest.

Tomorrow, we will tackle climbing a Himalayan giant, Annapurna, with its icy slopes. Meanwhile, we will check our supplies and rest.

To keep warm, we try to make tea; but at such an altitude, the water struggles to come to a boil. During the night, Kalsang, the group's Sherpa, heard some strange noises. Could it be the mysterious Yeti, which inspires so many legends?

Sherpa: An ethnic group originally from the mountainous region of Nepal. They work as guides and carriers for climbers of the Himalayas.

I can hardly believe it: I am actually in China!
It is the most ancient living civilization!
It is also the country with the largest
population in the world: 1.3 billion inhabitants.
One out of five people on earth is Chinese!

The minute I land at the airport, I am hit by the paradoxes of China. For
centuries, this country has developed independently from the rest of the world.
That's why everything here is so exotic, surprising, and strange. They keep close
ties with their ancestral culture in which dragons are well meaning and symbols
of good luck — they are represented pretty much everywhere.

This is a country where the environment is not a primary concern, but where the
last pandas live. A country where the political regime is communist, but the
economy is capitalist.

CHINA

中国

The panda has an iconic
status because this
unusual bear only lives
in the center of China,
amidst mountainous regions
covered with thick bamboo
forests, such as the
Sichuan Province.

北京地铁单程车票

完整车票当日乘车有效
请自觉遵守地铁规定

贰元
¥2.00

报销凭证   A157   014498

An old street in Shanghai during the monsoon.

A rice field in front of the Great Wall of China. A rice field is a set of water-flooded terraces where rice is grown. The Chinese have been cultivating rice since as far back as 8,000 BC, so they are masters at it. Found in every bowl, meal, and region, rice is a staple of the local diet.

The construction of the Great Wall, which is more than 5,000 miles (6,000 km) long, began under the Qin dynasty in the 3rd century BC, and continued for nearly 2,000 years. The purpose of this immense stronghold was to protect the empire against invasion from the nomadic Mongols to the north.
It is said to be the largest architectural structure ever built by mankind, and the only monument that is visible from the moon!

针灸穴位挂图

Chinese medicine has developed for centuries without any contact with Western science. This explains why it is so different from Western medicine. Acupuncture is one of the most original methods of Chinese medicine. It is based on the use of thin needles to poke the body in various areas. Each of these points is said to have an effect on the body.

霍門
章門
期門
天府
俠白
尺澤
孔最
急脈
陰廉
列缺
魚際
太淵
經渠
少商
中封
太衝
行間
大敦
膝關
曲泉
陰包
蠡溝
中都

Here I am in Japan, the illustrious "Land of the Rising Sun!" Reading about Japan in my childhood, I dreamed about the world of the Samurai, where courage and honor stood above all other values. This world, which was very real for centuries, has now been replaced by an ultra-modern civilization.

The Japanese may be proud of their innovative technology, but they still love to relive their past. In April, Hanami — the cherry blossom festival — gives Japanese a chance to stroll in magnificent parks and admire nature, dressed in their traditional kimonos.

Afterwards, everyone goes home to drink tea, according to an ancestral ritual, or to water their bonsai. A bonsai is a miniature, potted tree, with carefully trimmed branches. This requires daily attention, and it is a true passion for many Japanese folks.

The island of Komodo is home to giant lizards that make me wonder whether the dinosaur era is really over after all? Between 7 and 8 feet (2-3 m) long, weighing about 175 pounds (80 kilos), the Komodo dragon is the largest lizard on the planet.

Indonesia

With its blue sea backdrop and lush nature, Indonesia, a mosaic of approximately 18,000 islands and 210 million inhabitants, is the largest archipelago (group of islands) on earth. Sumatra is a land of impenetrable jungles, the realm of tigers, marmosets, orangutans, and small elephants; Borneo is filled with marvelous flowers and a huge biodiversity reserve; the isle of Java is spiked with volcanoes that are not quite completely asleep; Bali is also called "the Island of the Gods," due to its breathtaking beauty; and let's not forget Komodo and its rather scary lizards, plus Flores, Celebes, Timor, and thousands of other islands, all beautiful and ingrained with mystery and charm.

Australia is the largest island in the world. It is even a continent. I quickly leave the beautiful, large city of Sydney to meet Paddy Napurrula Nayowbolmi, my old aboriginal friend. He gives me a tour of wild Australia, also called the "outback."

We drive for a few days, hardly meeting a soul, aside from a small kangaroo tribe and a few koalas, before we finally reach the center of this land at the foot of the sacred aboriginal mountain, Uluru (Ayers Rock). Balandika, who is Paddy's cousin, introduces me to the difficult art of boomerang. Originally a hunting or war weapon, a boomerang always returns to its launcher when it misses its target, making it easy to use it again right away.

By nightfall, old Dhuwarrwou charms the spirits by blowing in his didgeridoo. The deep sound mesmerizes the audience, and that night dreams whisk me away into shamanic realms. The next morning, we say goodbye to Paddy's family; we are heading toward the tropical north, where I'm hoping to see the crocodiles.

AUSTRALIA

The Aborigines

Aborigines is the name given to Australia's first inhabitants. They probably reached the land about 50,000 years ago, when Australia was linked to Southeast Asia by a strip of land. Once the sea level rose, they remained isolated from the rest of the world until 1770, which is when the island was "discovered" by Captain Cook, who immediately claimed it as a British possession! When European immigrants arrived at the beginning of the 19th century, Aborigines practically disappeared—the victims of epidemics and massacres, as well as dispossession of their lands.

CROCODILE DUNDEE

THE AUSTRALIAN
DAILY PAPER

WEDNESDAY, APRIL 2, 2009   YOUR LOCAL NEWSPAPER   PHONE 9977 3333 80c INCL. GST

Shark attack !

NEXT
7 km

The great white shark terrorizes
Australian beaches.

BRAZIL

The word "Brazil" comes from the Latin word brasilium, which means "red embers." It refers to the glowing color of the wood that Portuguese seamen brought home with them in the 16th century. Brazil is the largest state in South America. It is also the only country on that continent where the national language is Portuguese. Once you leave the colorful and highly populated cities on the Atlantic Coast (Bahia, São Paulo, Rio de Janeiro and its famous Carnival) or Brasilia, the capital, you quickly find yourself in the largest rainforest on the planet: the Amazon (1,737,459 sq. mi or 4,500,000 km2).

AMAZONIA TOUR
8 dias na maior floresta do mund

Uma experiencia inesquecivel

In Brazil, futebol (soccer) is a true religion. With five World Cup victories (1958, 1962, 1970, 1994, and 2002) under its belt, this country boasts more titles than any other. Pelé, who played between 1958 and 1975, remains Brazil's most legendary player. But Ronaldo, Ronaldinho, and Kaká are the stars of today.

With 103,000 seats, the Maracanã stadium of Rio de Janeiro is one of the largest in the world.

Argentina is Brazil's great South American rival. Diego Maradona, its star player who goes by the nickname "El Pibe de Oro" (The Golden Kid), enchanted Argentinian supporters between 1980 and 1990.

Argentiiiiiiiina!

Correio do Brasil 0,50 RS

2002

Confederação Brasileira de Fute

400 PESOS

Argentiiiiina

REPÚBLICA ARGENTINA   CASA DE MON

ARGENTINIAN MEAT

It is considered one of the best in the world, because the animals are raised on open plains, completely free of hormones. Argentinian cows don't know what barns are—they graze in fields their whole life. That is why their meat is so delicious. Asado (beef grilled on charcoal) is the national dish. But wait! We're not talking about just any cut of meat on any fire, like a standard barbecue… This is about sharing enormous portions of meat with loved ones, savoring tender and juicy pieces simmered the unique Argentinian way!

In Argentina, the herdsmen in charge of the plain's herds are called "gauchos." The word is supposedly derived from the Quechua word *huacchu*, which means a "solitary person."

Argentina owes its name to the first Spanish conquistadors. Searching for gold in the region of Rio de la Plata (1516), they were welcomed by indigenous people, who presented them with gifts made of silver.

First a Spanish colony, Argentina conquered its independence in 1810 after "The May Revolution."

Many remember Juan Perón, who was in power between 1946 and 1955. But it is his spouse Eva Perón, fondly called Evita, who truly conquered the hearts of Argentinians. She died in 1952, but to this day, she is still the subject of legend and is worshiped as such.

Tango: A two-time dance born in Argentina at the end of the 19th century. The man guides the woman, who lets her weight sway naturally in the direction of the step. The church often banned the dance, finding it too passionate. Couples traditionally dance to the sound of a bandonéon (a type of accordion).

Not much remains, unfortunately, of the brilliant Inca civilization— just a few temples in ruins and stretches of walls in various parts of Peru.

My guide takes me to one of those temples lost in the jungle.

I sit down, grab my sketching gear, and try to imagine what these places were like at the glorious time of the Inca, who called themselves "sons of the sun."

Mysteries of the pre-Columbian Civilizations

The word "pre-Columbian" designates civilizations that flourished for centuries on the American continent before the arrival of Christopher Columbus.

The most well-known civilizations are the Inca (in Peru) and the Mayan, Aztec, Toltec, and Olmec (in Central America).

With the Spanish conquest in the 16th century, these brilliant civilizations faded away. Today, they remain shrouded in mystery, especially as far as archeology is concerned.

For instance, What happened to the Inca's treasure, which was hidden just before the conquistadors arrived? Is it buried deep under the waters of Lake Titicaca or hidden in inaccessible caves in the Andean Mountains?

Easter Island is yet another archaeological riddle. Situated 2,174 miles (3,500 km) from the coast of Chile, it was discovered on Easter Day in 1722. Immediately, the following question arose: Which incredible civilization could possibly have erected these gigantic statues, the famous "Moai" that are found on the island? →

The greatest mystery of all is probably the gigantic drawings on the ground at the Nazca site in Peru, which can only be seen from an airplane.

Eager to solve these archaeological mysteries, many authors have come up with bizarre explanations: extraterrestrial intervention, giants, magical and occult powers. Instead, we should recognize the inherent genius of these civilizations and accept that they were perfectly capable of hiding a treasure, erecting gigantic statues, or patiently drawing massive pictures on the ground.

Latin America

Latin America is the part of the American continent where the spoken languages are derived from Latin, such as: Spanish (Mexico, Argentina, Cuba, Bolivia, Columbia, etc.), Portuguese (Brazil), and French (Guadeloupe, Martinique, Guyana).

Aside from tourism and underground resources, a great part of the riches of Latin America come from agriculture, especially coffee, tobacco, sugar cane, and exotic fruits.

Butterfly (1906-1973): A famous inmate of the Cayenne prison who was sentenced to forced labor for life in 1931. He escaped and told his life story in a book called *Butterfly*. His real name is Henri Charrière, and his nickname came from the butterfly tattooed on his chest, as well as his desire for freedom.

The revolutionary Ernesto "Che" Guevara (1928-1967), who championed the cause of the peasants, is still an iconic figure in all of Latin America.

A tobacco plantation on a high plateau in the Andes.

The word "mariachi" designates both a group of musicians from Mexico and the style of music they play. This music is traditionally played during Mexican ceremonies and parties.

La Gran Fiesta Mexicana

MEXICO

Before its conquest by Hernán Cortés in 1519, the future state of Mexico was home to a great civilization: the Aztecs. According to their mythology, the god Quetzalcoatl appeared as a vulture near a lake, perched on a cactus and devouring a snake. The Aztecs decided to build a city there: Tenochtitlan, which later became Mexico City, one of the most populated cities in the world and the capital of Mexico.

Mexico has what it takes to charm tourists: beautiful beaches in Acapulco and Cancun, archaeological sites, popular culinary specialties (the famous guacamole, tacos, enchiladas, fajitas...), all of which contribute to make this beautiful country a top destination for visitors worldwide.

Sombrero: A typical Mexican hat. Its wide brim offers welcomed protection from the sun. The word derives from the Spanish word *sombra*, which means "shade, obscurity."

Two surfer friends: Phil "Good" Pinso and Frank "King" Fellous.

Shortboards appeared between 1960–1970. These lighter boards allow for better maneuverability and more speed.

Hawaii

The 50th state in the United States of America, Hawaii is an archipelago of 122 islands in the heart of the Pacific Ocean. Its capital is Honolulu, birthplace of American President Barack Obama.

Hawaii is a paradise for surfers, who are sure to find the biggest waves in the world here. As a matter of fact, between December to March, a giant wave break called "Jaws" unfolds in Peahi on the island of Maui. The giant waves, the highest on the planet, can reach 82 feet (25 meters)!

Even when there are no waves, the locals and the tourists still enjoy leisure time on the beach!

USA TODAY
NO. 1 IN THE USA

YES WE CAN !

The Declaration of Independence on July 4th, 1776. It is the national day of independence in the United States.

Dollar: North American money. It is the most widely used currency for worldwide transactions. The word "dollar" is an altered version of thaler, a silver currency that appeared at the beginning of the 16th century.

Barack Obama: The 44th and current president of the United States of America. He made history on November 4th, 2008, when he became the first African American president of the nation. He received the Nobel Peace Prize on October 9, 2009.

THE UNITED STATES OF

THIS NOTE IS LEGAL TENDER
FOR ALL DEBTS, PUBLIC AND PRIVATE

FIVE DOLLARS

TAXI

463 TAXI
1177/8822

Lunch at top of a Skyscraper (1932)

In Washington, D.C. and New York City

Along the East Coast of the United States of America are several large cities, including Washington, D.C. and New York City. Washington, D.C. is the political capital of the United States. This is where the president lives in the White House, and it is also home to the Parliament and the Capitol. The city owes its name to George Washington. He took an active part in the Revolutionary War in 1776 and then became the first president of the United States.

The political capital of Washington, D.C. coexists with the economic and cultural capital of New York City. I hop into a yellow cab, one of those famous taxis that roam the streets of the Big Apple, and I ask the cabbie to give me a tour.

My first stop is Wall Street, which is known as the financial center of the world. The world's most important banks have their headquarters there, and it is also home to the stock exchange. On Wall Street, it is common to see billionaires in sumptuous limousines and traders that are always in a hurry.

Time to visit the Museum of Modern Art, the "MOMA." After a quick walk in Central Park, a very large green space in the heart of Manhattan, I go up to the highest floor of the extraordinary skyscraper, the Empire State Building. From there, I have a panoramic view of the whole city. I am a bit disappointed, though, that I can't see King Kong anywhere! I kept the best for last: the famous Statue of Liberty, or "Miss Liberty," as the locals fondly call her. What a perfect name to symbolize the spirit of freedom of this great country...

INSERT THIS END UP

The Museum of Modern Art
Fri 5/29/09   1 entrance $ 9

The Statue of Liberty

Mount Rushmore, in South Dakota, is a monumental statue carved directly into a mountain. It depicts four great presidents in American history: George Washington, Thomas Jefferson, Theodore Roosevelt, and Abraham Lincoln.

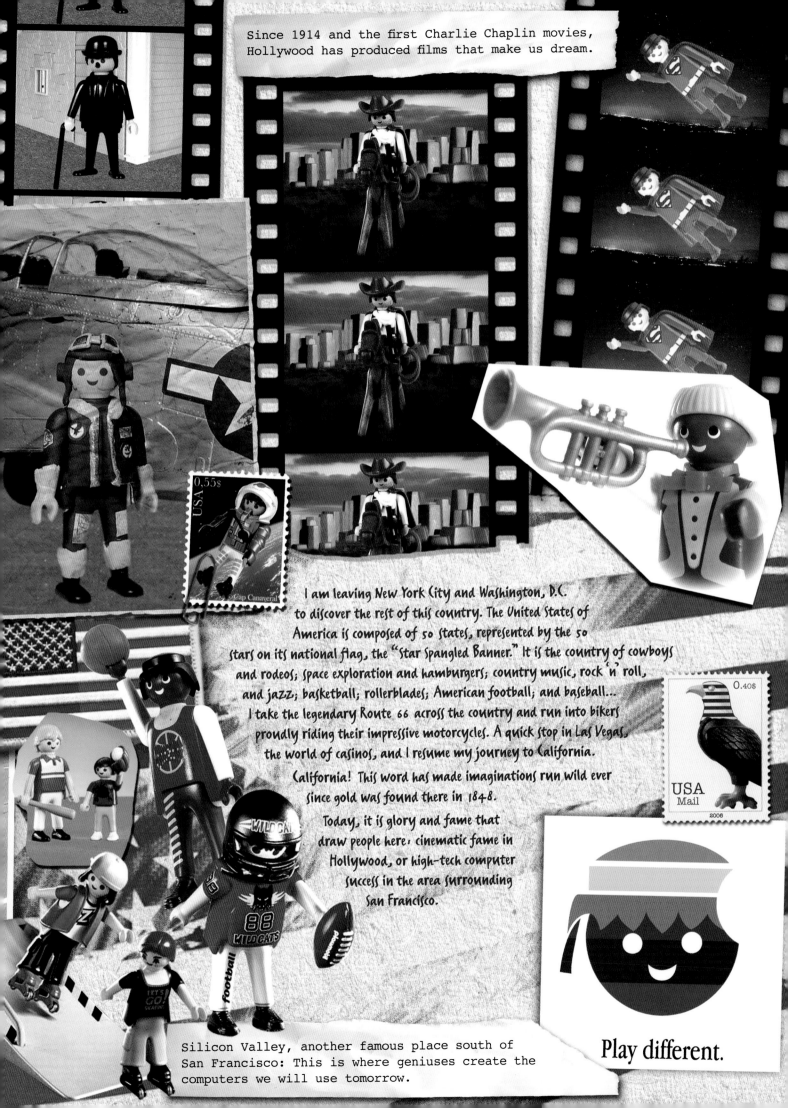

Since 1914 and the first Charlie Chaplin movies, Hollywood has produced films that make us dream.

I am leaving New York City and Washington, D.C. to discover the rest of this country. The United States of America is composed of 50 states, represented by the 50 stars on its national flag, the "Star Spangled Banner." It is the country of cowboys and rodeos; space exploration and hamburgers; country music, rock 'n' roll, and jazz; basketball; rollerblades; American football; and baseball... I take the legendary Route 66 across the country and run into bikers proudly riding their impressive motorcycles. A quick stop in Las Vegas, the world of casinos, and I resume my journey to California.

California! This word has made imaginations run wild ever since gold was found there in 1848.

Today, it is glory and fame that draw people here: cinematic fame in Hollywood, or high-tech computer success in the area surrounding San Francisco.

Silicon Valley, another famous place south of San Francisco: This is where geniuses create the computers we will use tomorrow.

Play different.

Canada is the second largest country in the world. However, it does not have a large population, as all of its major cities (the capital, Ottawa, as well as Quebec and Vancouver) are located in the south, along the border of the United States. The northern regions are almost deserted. Canada has nearly two million lakes, humongous rivers (Canada has the greatest freshwater reserve on the planet), and one of the largest forests in the world. Therefore, Canada produces large quantities of wood, in addition to its famous maple syrup—an absolute must with pancakes. As a matter of fact, the maple leaf is the national symbol of Canada.

An iconic figure of this country is its mounted police. Dressed in a red uniform and riding on horseback, they owe their fame to the gold rush at the end of the 19th century, a wild time during which maintaining order was very important.

Ice Hockey: A team sport that takes place in a skating ring. The aim is to score a goal by using a stick to shoot a rubber disk, called a puck, into the opponent's goal. The team is composed of a goalie and five players, with frequent player rotations. A high-speed sport, hockey has been called the "fastest sport in the world." It is the national Canadian sport, and the country took immense pride in earning a gold medal at the Vancouver Olympics in 2010.

The beaver became the official Canadian emblem in 1975.
With its reputation for patience and hard work, this large
rodent lives and thrives throughout the whole country.
Beavers are adept at building dams near fast-moving water,
which is how they earned their reputation.

Originally from Siberia, the husky is a small, sturdy, and tough dog, used by the Inuit people to drag loads or pull sleds.

As the finishing touch to my world tour, I am about to make one of my wildest dreams come true — to spend a few days in the extreme north with Inuit hunters on the ice packs, which are big areas of thick sheets of ice on the ocean.

Thanks to hunting and fishing, these people manage to survive in one of the most hostile environments in the world. Brrrrr! It is indeed cold, -22° Fahrenheit (- 30°C) when I exit the igloo where I spent the night, sheltered from the icy wind and snow.

Bundled up in blankets, I stay at the camp with the women and children while the men are away fishing, seal hunting, or whaling. I do my part to prepare the next meal, catching a few fish.

Ice Floe: An expanse of frozen sea that takes shape in the polar winter, when the water temperature goes below 28.4° Fahrenheit (-33.5°C). At the heart of winter, the ice can be 6½ feet (2 meters) thick, not counting the layer of snow on top. Nowadays, because of global warming, ice floes in the arctic region are diminishing drastically. Specialists worry about the consequences of this phenomenon—if nothing is done, they're afraid they might disappear for good!

Whaling

All sea animals, especially seals and whales, give the Inuit their livelihood: meat, grease, fur...

The Inuit

My deepest gratitude goes to my friend Bruno Peeters (aka Brubil), without whom this trip would not have been quite as beautiful. And a big hug to Edith and Sophie...

Many friends helped me achieve this tour of the world: the Moretti family, who offered me a wonderful limousine ride in New York; Patrick Danton (aka Master Fox), who took me to visit the Statue of Liberty; Daniele (aka Goldinca), who gave me beautiful documents about the Inca; Leopold and Dany, who were my tour guides in the pharaohs' Egypt; Lucie, for her spinning wheel—without it, Gandhi would not be Gandhi; Crystal, who took me on a Loch Ness tour in Scotland; Menes, who introduced me to a few old samurai; Kop, who guided me in Afghanistan; David Cantera, who took me to the movies to watch *Superman* in Los Angeles; Bhinomura, who helped me find Charlie; Laurent Chassard, who loaned me his plane to fly over Nazca; Paul Lo, who took me along in his fishing boat; and Duhamel, who made me discover the minotaur. I also want to thank Freddo, Menes, and Captain Playmo for lending me comics that proved very entertaining during long layovers. I also want to thank the websites planeteplaymo.net, playmoboys.com, tricornejock.com, playmoboard.com, playmofriends.com, klickywelt.de, playclicks.com, and aesclick.com—these are top-notch travel agencies in the land of Playmobil, and their talented members are a constant source of inspiration.

I want to extend my thanks to my Playmobil fan friends, who helped me during my adventures: Teddyboy, Claude Hengel, Cooster, René Ducasse, Macgayver, Tophe, Michel Sbraire, Stéphane, Wyser, ben-g2, Luis, Sleepy, Ginger, Laurent alias Fiplay, Poney73, Foulques de playmoléon, Dudulle, Tricornejock, Fanny & Olivier, Virgin, Marmotte, Alain Gibert, David Obadia, Emile Rouze, Erwan Le Vexier, Kevin Sabbah, Gies Proesmans, Playmoboys D2, Javier Pascual, Jordi Carpio Rojas, and all those I may have forgotten to mention.

Thank you to the Brandstätter Group, especially Andrea Schauer, Iris Herold, Ligia Nirestean, and Sylvia Gerlach, for helping me cross the borders of the Playmobil world.

VENEZIA

MEMORIA DI ROMA

BRUXELLES

مصر

By the same author...

The mystery of *Sherlock Holmes: The Hound of the Baskervilles* comes to life in this Playmobil world. Follow along as Sherlock Holmes meets interesting characters and uses his amazing detective skills and instincts to solve a crime!

Quarto is the authority on a wide range of topics.
Quarto educates, entertains and enriches the lives of our readers—
enthusiasts and lovers of hands-on living.
www.quartoknows.com

6 Orchard Road, Suite 100
Lake Forest, CA 92630
quartoknows.com
Visit our blogs @quartoknows.com

Translated by Sophie Raimondo, AAA French Translations.

© 2015 by geobra Brandstätter Stiftung & Co. KG, Zirndorf/Germany
® PLAYMOBIL pronounced; plāy - mõ - bēel
www.playmobil.com
licensed by: BAVARIA MEDIA, www.bavaria-media.de

original French edition © Casterman, 2010
www.casterman.com

Casterman Editions
47 Cantersteen, boite 4
1000 Bruxelles